Mascot

Jon Dowling
Counter-Print

A Moment for the Mascot

Designing an engaging and memorable mascot isn't easy but, once you get to grips with what makes a good mascot great, it certainly does get easier. Often the best place to start is to look back to those you remember fondly and try to decipher why it was that you fell in love with them in the first place.

① Hodori, 1988 Seoul Olympic
Olympic mascot

② Scottie, the Netto dog logo

③ Lacoste logo

One of my earliest memories of being aware of 'branding' was at seven years old when my uncle, recently back from a business trip to the Far East, handed me a t-shirt with a dancing tiger on the front. It was easily my favourite t-shirt at the time, to the point at which all other garments were consigned to my cupboard on a permanent basis and this one would happily stay on until it would either fall off or become grafted to my skin, leaving me with a rather fetching 'Hodori' the tiger tattoo.

Hodori ① was the official mascot of the 1988 Summer Olympic games in Seoul, South Korea, and it was easy to fall in love with him. The stylised tiger was designed by Kim Hyun as an amiable Armur tiger, meant to portray the friendly and hospitable traditions of the Korean people. The name 'Hodori' was chosen from over 2,000 suggestions sent in by the public at the time: 'Ho' deriving from the Korean word for 'tiger' ('horangi') and 'dori' a diminutive for 'boys' in Korea.

In hindsight, I never had a chance not to fall in love with him, did I? The whole Hodori package was so tailor-made for a boy of seven, from its name to its characterisation, that I had no choice but to buy into the little tiger, who was seemingly throwing a peace sign and streaming a letter 'S' from an inexplicable ribbon on its cap.

Hodori was a formidable marketing tool, both for the games themselves and, importantly for any Olympic event, the outward perception of the country holding them. Animal mascots in general can be extremely effective marketing tools; able to simultaneously disarm us with their charm and influence us with their character, spirit and attitude.

Interest in the animal as a logo or symbol dates way back in the history of art, past Tony the Tiger or the Netto dog ② to the caves of Lascaux in France and the hieroglyphics of ancient Egypt. Since the dawn of creation, we have painted, engraved and used animals as signs of astrology and magic, adopted their forms in our writing and symbols, alphabets, coats of arms, pennants and banners.

It was only later that, in recent history, animals were utilised and adapted in the advertising and design world to meet commercial purposes. From the latter half of the 20th Century, until now, the range and proliferation of brand names and iconography on clothing and sports goods, for example, has produced so many animal logos that it is difficult to imagine the world today without them – from Puma to Slazenger; from Ralph Lauren to Lacoste. ③

The Lacoste brand is full of history. Its founder, René Lacoste, was a professional tennis player in the early 20th century; the winner of 10 grand slam tennis tournaments. He invented the signature polo shirt because he wanted something more comfortable to wear in competitions than the long-sleeved shirts of the time. An American journalist gave Lacoste the nickname 'The Alligator' after overhearing him make a bet with his coach, over an alligator-skin suitcase, that he would win the Davis Cup in Boston. When he returned to France, 'alligator' became 'crocodile' and the tennis star asked his friend Robert George to design a corresponding logo for him.

As with Lacoste, the naming of an establishment, business or sports team can often naturally lead to an animal mascot. The product in which one trades can also be a determining factor in choosing an animal. Often the choice of mascot reflects a desired quality; a common example of this is the 'fighting spirit', in which a competitive nature is characterised by a predatory animal.

Companies use characters as logos or mascots, whether in animal or human form, because they create a physical face

④ The Jolly Green Giant

⑤ Monsier Bibendum
(The Michelin Man), Michelin

for customers. People gravitate towards their familiar features and they can be made to be gender specific, as in the case of the Jolly Green Giant;⑧ or age specific, as in the case of my little friend Hodori. The character, however, should never detract attention from the company. Rather, if done well, a product or service of the company can be alluded to within the mascot as a statement of the company's purpose.

Mascots often have an integrated thought process behind them, a storyline or motive for their existence, and the mascot can take on a variety of forms depending on the company they represent. One of my favourite mascots and character logos has got to be Michelin's 'Monsier Bibendum'⑧ who was first born as a concept at the World Exhibition of Lyon in 1894. There Edouard Michelin, the founder of the company, saw a pile of automobile tyres that were wrapped in fabric. 'If they just had arms and legs, then they would look like a human being,' he thought to himself and, in the next breath, he thought of a poster that showed a fat Bavarian with a beer in his hand which had a headline in Latin: 'Nunc est bibendum!' or 'Now it's time to drink!' Putting these two images together, Michelin then had a poster

designed with what can only be described as a 'tyre-man' holding a glass with nails and shards. Its message was 'Now it's time to drink! To your health! Michelin tyres swallow every obstacle!', thus implying that you can drive over anything with them.

The lovable and familiar figure was first conceived more than a century ago and is still going strong today; it's hard to think of too many mascots from that time which have aged so well, while continuously evolving and reinventing themselves.

Times have obviously changed since the advent of Monsier Bibendum or even the momentary appearance of Hodori the tiger on the world stage in 1988. This can be clearly seen through the design of subsequent Olympic mascots.

Olympic mascots have been a key part of the Games since 1968. They're tasked with giving concrete form to the Olympic spirit, spreading the values highlighted at each edition of the Games; promoting the history and culture of the host city and giving the event a festive atmosphere. Many have become celebrated for their design and communicative value, such as Waldi⑧ from the 1972 Munich games or Cobi, the 1992 Barcelona Olympics mascot.

Companies use characters as logos or mascots because they create a physical face for customers.

⑥ Waldi, 1972 Munich
Olympic mascot

⑦ Wenlock, 2012 London
Olympic mascot

⑧ Miraitowa, 2020 Tokyo
Olympic mascot

We had our own shot at it in 2012 with Britain's own Wenlock ⑦ and Mandeville, designed by Iris. The two characters were this time named after Much Wenlock in Shropshire, the village that hosted a precursor to the Olympics in the 19th century, and Stoke Mandeville hospital, the birthplace of the Paralympic Games. Each mascot sported a yellow light on top of its head as a reference to London's black cabs and the Olympic Rings got a nod via Wenlock's bracelets – as they did with Hodori's medal around his neck.

They were a far cry from Hodori's traditional cartoon-like style, which I imagine would have felt pretty comfortable and safe, even in 1988. The new mascots, seemingly, were meant to represent the aspirations and enthusiasm of children in 2012 towards the Olympic Games. They had their own Twitter feeds and were designed to be viewed on social media, computer screens and YouTube; not just on printed material or a seven-year-old's t-shirt. Fast-forward another eight years and we were introduced to Tokyo's 2022 mascot 'Miraitowa'. ⑧ Designed by Ryo Taniguchi, its name derived from the Japanese words 'mirai' (future) and 'towa' (eternity). This name was chosen to promote a, 'future full of eternal hope in the hearts of people all over the world'. Lofty ambitions for a cartoon cat.

With its traditional and futuristic style, the mascot embodied both the old and the new, echoing the concept of 'innovation from harmony'. Miraitowa and his sidekick Someity were turned into robots for the games. Programmed to show facial expressions, they were designed to wave and shake hands with fans. A plan that would be made somewhat redundant by an unforeseen global pandemic.

Both the 2012 and 2020 mascots had their detractors – 2012's Wenlock and Mandeville where considered not cuddly enough, while Tokyo's Miraitowa and

Someity received some criticism for the use of blue and pink characterisation and the mascots falling clearly into traditional gender roles.

Some form of backlash towards mascots for global events has come to be expected. After all, we all have our favourites when we look back with nostalgia. However, I prefer to put a positive spin on it and, as a fan of mascots, I think it's comforting to know that they are still with us, fighting their corner as a mainstay of graphic design, with today's design talent daring to re-invent them to meet the needs of our times.

The work within this book, indicates that their popularity has certainly not diminished over time. If anything, they seem to be having a bit of a moment, co-opted to help sell or promote anything from tech companies and financial organisations to burger chains, record fairs and publishers

Part of their charm must be their variety. A 'mascot' can be either a person, animal or object and they are usually thought to bring luck. Simple and playful like Hodari, or sophisticated and current like Wenlock and Mandeville, Miraitowa and Someity, mascots are fun characters that manage to put a smile on your face and simultaneously stand for something – injecting meaning and playfulness into a brand and creating a lasting impression.

I hope you like the examples we have collated here in 'Mascot'. They represent the most interesting, considered and often fun representations of the art form we could find from contemporary branding agencies. We'd like to take this opportunity to thank the designers for their time, support and talent.

Jon Dowling
Counter-print

People

Newspaper Club

D8 / d8.studio

D8 have worked with Newspaper Club since 2015. Their first collaboration was helping Newspaper Club refresh their brand, which involved drawing a new version of their paperboy mascot, Russell. He was inspired by classic 1950s mascots such as Mister Minit, but with a more contemporary flair. Over the years D8 have designed various goodies like print samples, postcards, badges, and stickers. More importantly this means D8 have spent plenty of time with Russell, reimagining him in different outfits and scenarios that add a friendly face and inject some personality into the Newspaper Club brand.

PRINT SOMETHING

✌ D8 have spent plenty of time with Russell, reimagining him in different outfits and scenarios that add a friendly face and inject some personality into the Newspaper Club brand. ✌

Gender Creative Kids

Wedge / wedge.work

Since 2013, Gender Creative Kids Canada has provided education, community, resources, and services towards the affirmation of trans, non-binary, and gender creative youth among their families, schools, and society at large.

In 2019, the non-profit organisation's Board of Directors invited Wedge to join as their official brand partner to design their visual identity. Wedge sought to honour GCKC's work with a visual expression that officialises their position on a global stage and uses design as a tool for understanding.

This work is rooted in values of human dignity, inclusivity, community, empathy, and joy, as well as informed by workshops and educational training graciously given to the Wedge team by GCKC. Design choices are intentional, beyond aesthetics. White space is integrated as a key colour, as it is in this undefinable space that we are able to freely discover who we are. This is complemented by an optimistic palette that is fluid, flexible, and approved by the kids.

An iconic character came to life as the symbol of the organisation, inspired by the truest part of you: the heart. Standing tall and confident with a look of optimism, always moving forward. It's in these thoughtful details that Wedge arrive at a solution that can only be Gender Creative Kids.

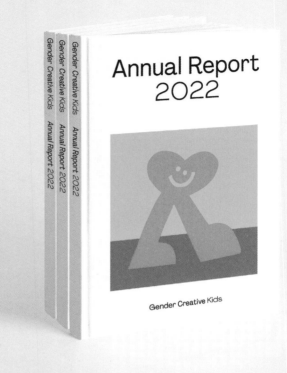

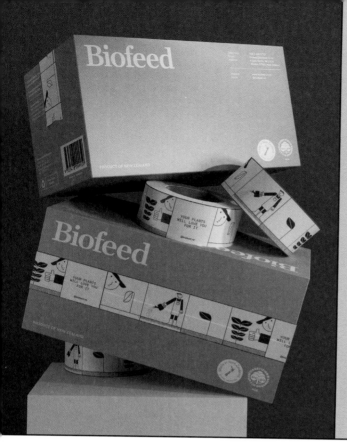

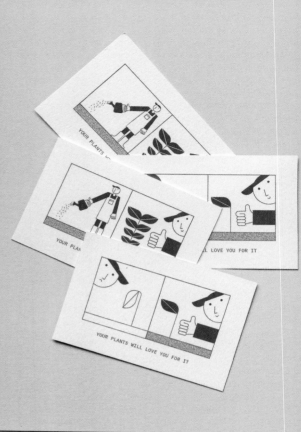

Biofeed

makebardo / makebardo.com

Biofeed has been satisfying gardeners in New Zealand since 1994 with their high-quality, nutritionally balanced, certified organic compost tea.

They approached makebardo to redesign their brand because they needed to clearly show, through their identity, the values of their product. Since this is an organic product, it has a genuinely positive impact, and the result of using it is highly effective. makebardo's challenge was to create a brand narrative capable of showing the product's effectiveness and the principles of the company, with a simple and clear message.

makebardo worked with the concept 'Before & After' to highlight how the product performs. In order to avoid visual clichés around this theme, they looked at the world of comics so that they could communicate the company's story through fun and engaging vignettes.

The result is singular and cohesive, but above all, it is flexible because it combines the comic vignettes to create multiple outcomes, achieving a memorable brand experience.

YOUR PLANTS WILL LOVE YOU FOR IT

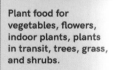
Plant food for
vegetables, flowers,
indoor plants, plants
in transit, trees, grass,
and shrubs.

Benefits: Safe and easy to use / No unpleasant odors / Environmentally friendly / Promotes healthy roots and plants / Aids plant's immune system against pests and diseases / Not harmful on skin contact.

Feeding: Soak seedling (either singly or whole punnet), plant, rose, shrub, tree or indoor plant roots in Biofeed solution for 10-20 minutes prior to planting. After planting, water in with solution. This will aid against transplant shock and disease.

Foliar Spray: Use Biofeed solution weekly or fortnightly as required until fruiting or flowering begins. This will enhance stem and plant health. In hot weather spray in early mornings and late evenings only. For spray recipes please see brochure or website.

Germinating: Sow seeds into trays. Feed with Biofeed solution weekly. When seeds appear, use Biofeed foliar spray with each watering.

PRODUCT OF NEW ZEALAND   @biofeed.nz #aampuifou

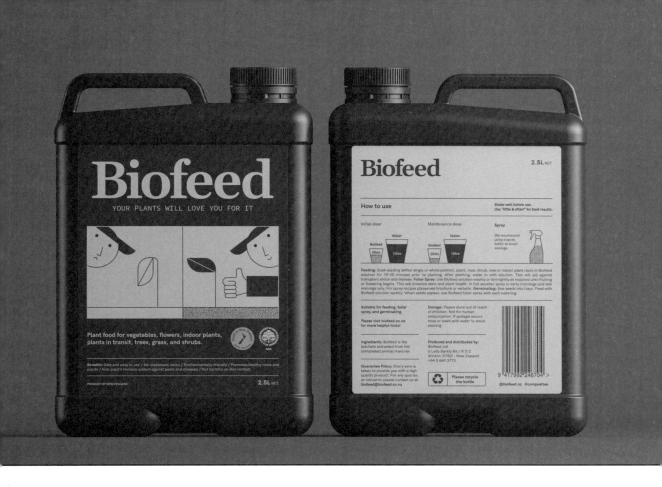

☝ makebardo's challenge was to create a brand narrative capable of showing the product's effectiveness and the principles of the company, with a simple and clear message. ✌

Remedial Massage

makebardo / makebardo.com

Remedial Massage provide massage therapy treatments tailored to the individual. Generally in the field of health, tone of voice is impersonal and colloquial. Remedial Massage had to be different in order to attract new patients and cultivate loyalty. makebardo's idea was to break the communications norm for this industry, with a deep sense of humour.

The tagline, 'In like a pretzel, out like a noodle', was created to convey the idea of a 'before' and an 'after', reflecting the concept of recovery. makebardo evolved the word-mark, pictorial mark and illustrated characters.

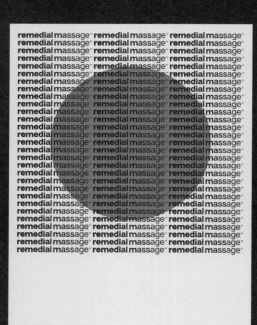

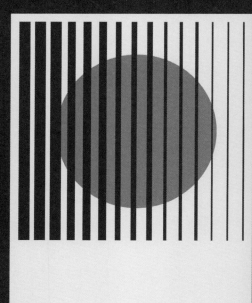

Parliament of Catalonia

Requena / andresrequena.es
In 2020 the Parliament of Catalonia commemorated the 40th anniversary of the restoration of democracy together with its citizens.

The Parliament already had an identity that contained the fundamental values of commitment and plurality. The challenge for Requena was to appropriate, accentuate and consolidate its representative connotations, in a formal allegory of the Parliament, while adding a new meaning that contained and projected the specific weight of the anniversary.

Employment Hero

Twist / designbytwist.com

Employment Hero is an HR, payroll and people management platform. Designed to make employment easier and more rewarding for everyone, the platform guides SME's along the path to success by powering productivity. In repositioning them, Twist brought the 'hero' to life. Working with artist Alec Doherty, Twist created a brand character as an advocate for better employment – personifying the mission and amplifying their message. A new graphic language, distilled from the logo, serves as a dynamic framing element, while a direct brand voice challenges conventional notions of employment, championing a better way.

👌 **Working with artist Alec Doherty, Twist created a unique brand character as an advocate for better employment.** 🤞

ADG Laus Awards

Requena / andresrequena.es

With more than 50 years of experience, the ADG Laus Awards have established themselves as the leading awards for graphic design and visual communication in Spain. Each year they recognise the best projects, in five categories: graphic design, digital, advertising, audiovisual and students. Their aim is to promote design and project its cultural, social and economic importance.

The first reference for this call for entries were cartoons, where the villain always loses. In this case, Requena changed the narrative. When the costumed villain realises that chasing the 'good guy' is not going to bring him tangible benefits, he suddenly finds the reward and both parties win. This story, taken to the world of communication, hides a double message; that good ideas are rewarded and that these ideas do not necessarily have to come from the predictable side, the villain or the hero.

Win Win

Cambia de idea. Cambia el mundo.

⊷

51a Edició dels Premis ADG Laus de Disseny Gràfic i Comunicació Visual
Inscripcions fins el 01.03.21 — Enviament del material fins el 11.03.21

51ª Edición de los Premios ADG Laus de Diseño Gráfico y Comunicación Visual
Inscripciones hasta el 01.03.21 — Envío del material hasta el 11.03.21

Call for Entries

Institucions: Generalitat de Catalunya, Ajuntament de Barcelona

Col·laboradors Premium: Moritz, Agpograf, Unión Papelera, Ojo de Nadal

Extra Nice

Animade / animade.tv

Animade are known the world over for their characterful animation and playful approach, so when champions of creativity It's Nice That were making an identity for their new membership offering, a partnership was born.

It's Nice That developed the Extra Nice logo mark and website, while Animade took care of the visual assets across the brand, including character design and the core identity film.

The character's simple blocky shapes, big hands and solid feet speak to its utility and generosity; they stand firm as a kind, supportive character. But they are also inquisitive and welcoming, they love to express themselves, and they are, of course, utterly playful.

Steve Gavan

Steve Gavan
stevegavan.work

Life. Be in it.™
① Life Be In It by Alex Stitt

slip!
slop!
slap!

② Sid the Seagull by Alex Stitt

Q   What is your background and how did you become involved in graphic design/illustration?

A   I was lucky enough to know I wanted to be a graphic designer from a young age. I was drawn to bold, colourful imagery and fun typography. After studying a Bachelor of Design at university, I jumped straight into studio work where I learnt the ropes. I spent the next eight years in the industry before working up my illustration skills. I find approaching illustration with an understanding of design makes it easier for me to dissect a brief and think strategically as well as creatively.

Q   How would you describe your creative style and process?

A   I like to ask a lot of questions to get a really strong understanding of the business and audience before I start conceptualising. I usually kick the process off with research, referencing old and often overlooked designs, like fruit stickers, packaging and signage for inspiration. I sketch up initial ideas and seek client feedback early, I find working collaboratively results in a solution that both the client and I are happy with.

Q   What do you think makes a successful mascot?

A   I think the most important thing is that it's memorable and emotive, so it really conveys what the brand is about in a distinctive way.

Q   Do you have a favourite mascot and why?

A   Being an Australian kid in the 90s, I was surrounded by some amazing Aussie mascots. One that really resonated with me was 'Life Be In It'® by Alex Stitt – a campaign that encouraged Aussies to get active and exercise. Alex Stitt had another great mascot named Sid the Seagull® that taught kids to 'Slip, Slop, Slap', i.e. be sun smart by slipping on a tee shirt, slopping on some sunscreen and slapping on a hat. Both mascots used humour in a laid back, fun way to communicate their message.

Thanks to Sid I was never sun burnt!

Q   We've been using mascots in branding for the last 100 years, why do you think they have stood the test of time?

④ Tex, the Alamo mascot
by Steve Gavan

Bloom Street mascot
by Steve Gavan

A   For me a mascot can encapsulate everything about a brand in one, succinct, emotive visual. They also have the ability to evolve overtime, growing and changing as their audience does.

Q   What was your experience with designing the Alamo mascot?

A   The Alamo mascot was one of the first mascots I designed and was for a pop-up bar in Brisbane, Australia. Like any branding brief, this one came with challenges – the mascot (named Tex) needed to communicate a western-style saloon vibe, while being flexible enough to convey each of the bar's venues and feel like he was constantly on-the-move. A lot to sum up in one image!

Q   Do you have any specific hopes for how this mascot will develop?

A   Alamo has had a couple of years off due to the pandemic. The plan is that, once they start up again, they'll find a new location every summer. I want Tex to grow and change to fit every new environment, and ensure that he brings a sense of positivity and humour to each pop-up.

Q   What are your main goals and considerations when working on a mascot?

A   My goals are always to make my mascots unique, fun and memorable, while also taking into consideration the brief criteria, the location, culture and brand values of the business and who I'm trying to reach in terms of target market. Obviously, I also want to make the process enjoyable for me too, so injecting fun and joy into each illustration is key.

Q   How can a mascot enhance a brand?

A   A mascot is a great way of communicating a brand's tone quickly and easily in a visual way. Anything that can be digested succinctly and clearly is going to help a brand's effectiveness and approachability.

A mascot can encapsulate everything about a brand in one, succinct, emotive visual. They also have the ability to evolve overtime, growing and changing as their audience does.

Alamo

Steve Gavan / stevegavan.work
Alamo is a western, saloon-style, pop-up whiskey bar that opens in a different location every year in Brisbane, Australia. They required a logo that reflected their country aesthetic and a mascot that suggested they won't be open for long and are always on the move.

Bloom Street

Steve Gavan / stevegavan.work

Bloom Street is an international sales and distribution agency for designer object and homeware brands. With offices located in Los Angeles, Sydney and London, Bloom Street aims to deliver beautiful products to homes around the world. Steve Gavan created this fun and friendly mascot to match the modern, playful pieces on offer.

TeeDesign

TeeDesign

Tais Kahatt / taiskahatt.com

TeeDesign is a marketplace for independent artists to sell their work on high-quality t-shirts.
They invite creators to express their passion and share them with the world. In that sense, as a
consumer, no matter how weird, niche or subcultural you're looking for, they have something for you.
The idea of the brand is to reflect that, and the t-shirt mascot shows exactly what the brand is all
about, the possibility to show your creations – a t-shirt with a voice.

Obby

Koto / koto.studio

Obby challenges adults to rethink learning. Far from tedious evening classes or throwaway experiences, they provide a hands-on way to develop skills while having fun with a community of interested people.

To represent its full spectrum of subjects and personalities, Obby's multidisciplined mascots carry oversized tools to show off their creative talents.

These faceless friends put their interests front and centre, inviting others to partake in pottery, piano or photography without preconceptions of ability or background. Doubling as badges, each character represents a different accomplishment, motivating learners to hone their skills in a particular subject or try something else entirely.

👌 **To represent its full spectrum of subjects and personalities, Obby's multidisciplined mascots carry oversized tools to show off their creative talents.** ✌️

Pringles

Jones Knowles Ritchie / jkrglobal.com
The new Pringles identity puts Mr P. front and centre. JKR elevated this much loved and distinctive mascot, referencing elements from the past whilst focussing on making the icon fit for the future to connect with consumers today.

With a new haircut, an expressive pair of eyebrows and an oversized red bow tie (containing an updated wordmark), the new design seeks to give Mr P. a new lease of life across the entire brand experience.

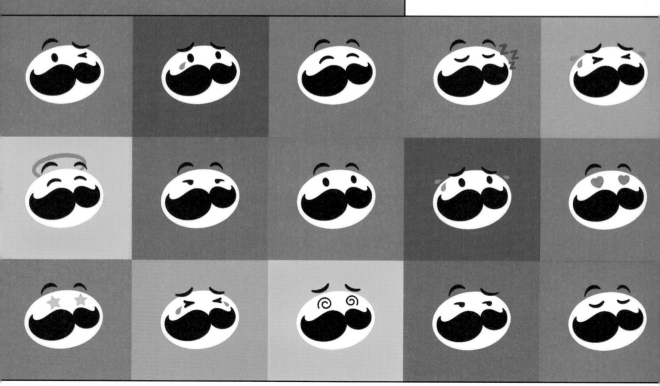

Feria

PAZ MIAMOR / pazmiamor.com

Feria juices are a sub-brand produced by Cafería, a specialty coffee shop. Feria sticks to Cafería's identity, which is based on illustrated characters in urban situations that do not refer to the product. These characters focus on the experience rather than the product, leaving open the possibility of labelling different types of products in the future.

Feria's intention is to bring local and healthy products to a young audience, adding value to the main brand, but above all, promoting healthy values in a fun and relaxed way.

Sweety Ripple

HDU[23] Lab / hdu23.design

Sweety Ripple is a new brand of tea drinks and its main product is fresh fruit tea. In the visual design of the brand, HDU[23] Lab established a wave movement within the design system to echo the brand name Sweety Ripple. They then illustrated witty facial expressions to help establish an emotional communication with consumers and convey a sense of satisfaction. Finally, HDU[23] Lab used pictures of raw materials without modification and unconventional typesetting without information hierarchy to reflect that the product was fresh and additive-free. There is no logo, in the traditional sense. In the visual design of Sweety Ripple, information, illustration and photography is combined in a wavy format, to create a unique and memorable brand visual.

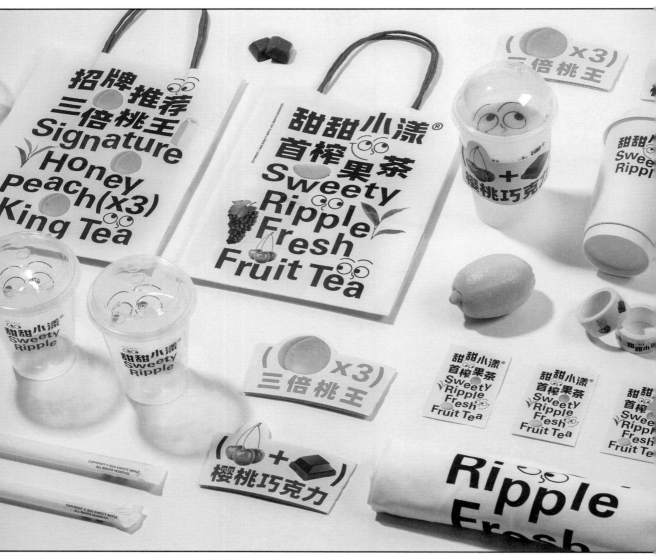

甜甜小漾® 首榨果茶

Sweety Ripple

Fresh Fruit Tea

招牌樱桃巧克力

Cherry Chocolate Smoothie

精选土耳其樱桃

Selected Cherry from Turkey

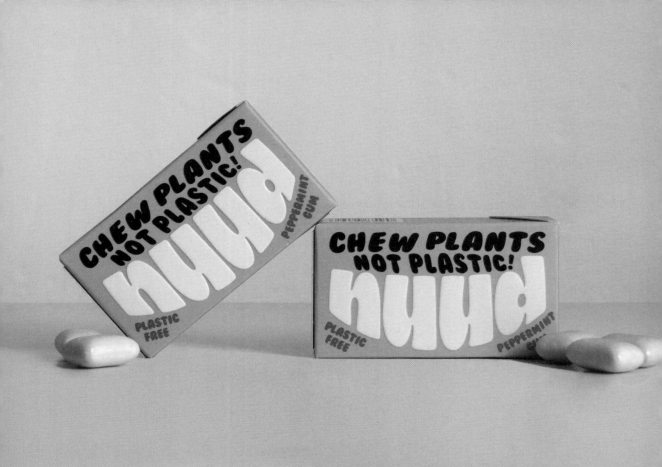

Nuud

Mother Design / motherdesign.com
Nuud is a plant-based, plastic free, biodegradable, sugar free and vegan chewing gum. In an otherwise polluting category, all of these things make for a revolutionary new gum. It's sugar free, vegan and tastes great.

Mother Design developed a brand language that's fearless but also light-hearted. It uses a new, iconic Nuud logo to its full potential on packaging and features a nude, gender neutral mascot 'Charlie', the brand's spokesperson, who helps communicate their important message successfully, in a playful and distinctive way.

STOP CHEWING PLASTIC

gum with nothing to ~~fill~~ ~~polluting~~

#CHEWPLANTSNOTPLASTIC

nuud

👆 **Nuud is a plant-based, plastic free, biodegradable, sugar free and vegan chewing gum. In an otherwise polluting category, all of these things make for a revolutionary new gum.** ✌

Andrés Requena

Requena
andresrequena.es

① Benny, the Chicago Bulls mascot

② Curro, 1992 Seville Expo mascot by Heinz Edelmann

Q   What is your background and how did you get into graphic design?

A   I studied in Barcelona and graduated in graphic design at Bau School. During my professional career I worked as a graphic designer, copywriter and art director for large agencies and design studios. Requena Office was born in 2014, betting on a reduced format to enhance the complicity with the client, the control over the process, the excellence in the result and an integral, resolute and transparent service.

Q   How would you describe your style and creative process?

A   We always use experiences and storytelling as a process. Mental images are built from a multitude of experiences and references that over time are reduced to the essential, that's why they remain, that's why they are not forgotten, like memories. For us, in any design process, the fundamental thing is to create and identify the images that define and transcend from those that only lead to common places. We believe in the concept as an objective

and in graphic expression as a consequence. Our vision flees from gimmicks to embrace vibrant and seductive visual solutions with relevance in time, that remain, that are not forgotten. As memories.

Q   What do you think makes a successful mascot?

A   Mascots are a much closer and corporeal extension of the brand. In a way they are literally the tangible representation of a brand. A mascot can shake your hand, a logo cannot.

Q   Do you have a favourite mascot and why?

A   I grew up watching Michael Jordan's Bulls so their mascot, Benny the Bull, ① was very funny to me. I also think it was pure contrast. The image we have of the bull in Spain is associated with bullfighting, with its epicness and the Bulls mascot was a funny bull that did incredible dunks. But my favourite is undoubtedly Curro, ② the mascot of the Expo'92 in Seville. When a mascot works, it quickly becomes an

Mag, the Café el Magnífico mascot by Requena

Sans, the Sans & Sans mascot by Requena

icon. In this case, I would say an evocative symbol of a generation and an era.

Q   We have been using mascots in branding for 100 years, why do you think they have stood the test of time?

A   I think it is because they are a very useful element to show brands in a much closer way, to create empathy. On many occasions mascots have also been misused to try to whitewash or clean up a brand, something that doesn't usually work.

Q   What is your experience with designing your mascots, is it a difficult process?

A   Mascots should be created to present a much more open and dynamic scenario, an imagery that feeds the fun version of the brand, so the process should be just as enjoyable. All our mascots are born to generate positive impact and this is how they have been created.

Q   Do you have any specific hopes for the evolution of mascots in the future?

A   I think the mascot world has had ups and downs and, at times, a certain degree of over-saturation but in the end the mascots that best connect with people will survive.

Q   What are your main goals and considerations when working on a mascot?

A   To create stories that otherwise could not be told or would be much more difficult. The mascot always has to be at the service of the story and not the other way around.

Q   How can a mascot enhance a brand?

A   I believe that the use of mascots should be an extra complement to add value to a brand that works and is already established, not as a replacement or a substitute.

I believe that the use of mascots should be an extra complement to add value to a brand that works and is already established, not as a replacement or a substitute.

Mag by El Magnifico

Requena / andresrequena.es

Café el Magnífico wanted to strategically reposition itself and update its visual universe to reach a diverse target. Requena started with the partial reduction of its name to introduce Mag, a character that brought together the brand values and projected them through messages and situations which relate to the world of coffee.

Sans by Sans & Sans

Requena / andresrequena.es

Requena followed the strategy of Café el Magnífico (opposite page) for Sans & Sans. Partially reducing the name, they created another character that acts as a visual ambassador to carry the weight of the discourse and brand messages. In this way Requena activated and graphically linked two identities, providing visibility and narrative recognition between them and their related products.

Brewbike

Koto / koto.studio

Supporting tomorrow's leaders through cold brew coffee is Brewbike's mission. Born on a college campus, they empower students to start micro-businesses and build life skills that serve them beyond graduation.

A business grounded in college culture naturally needs its own mascot. Enter Brew Bean, a caffeinated character embodying all the positive characteristics of Brewbike's teammates.

The main mascot co-exists with 50 other expressive beans, representing the various schools and personalities behind Brewbike. With new locations continually added, universities create their own bespoke beans, kitted out with iconic objects that authentically represent their college.

Nud

Maniac Studio / behance.net/maniacstudio
Few things compare to the sensation of the first sip
of a good cup of coffee or the first bite of a delicious
bun; hence the concept of the Nud brand is born.
It all begins from that first sip or bite that makes you
feel as if nothing else exists, there is no rush, there are
no troubles, other people, it's just you, 'nude', enjoying
a brief moment of happiness.

For the visual identity, Maniac Studio designed a
series of characters that portray the love for coffee,
bread and those pleasant sensations we feel when
tasting them. The feeling of the brand is soft, cute and
casual. It is a brand that communicates in 'diminutive',
a manner of speaking in Mexico, the things we care
and enjoy the most.

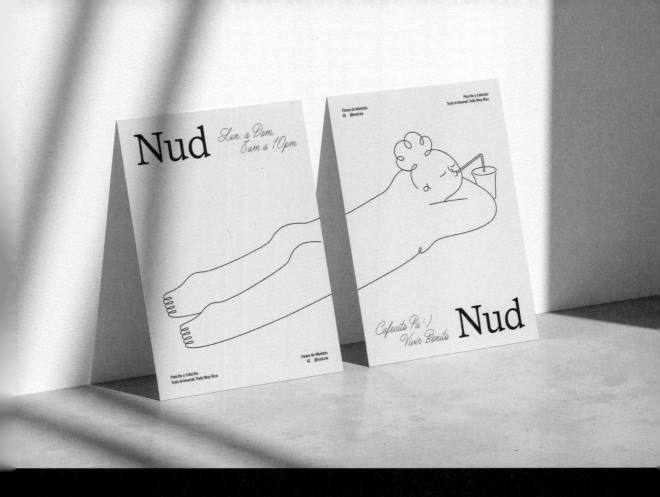

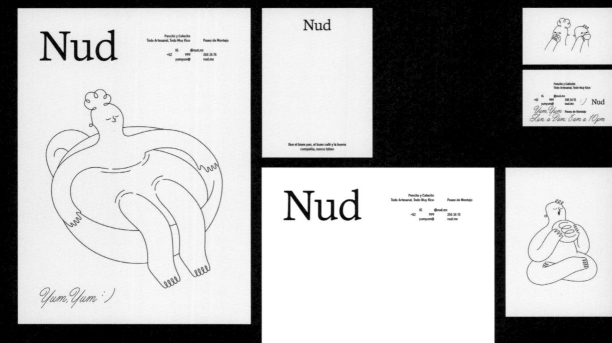

✌️ **For the visual identity, Maniac Studio designed a series of characters that portray the love for coffee, bread and those pleasant sensations we feel when tasting them.** ✌️

Gene & Georgetti

Paperwhite Studio / paperwhite-studio.com
Gene & Georgetti was founded in 1941. Legends like
Frank Sinatra, Bob Hope, and Lucille Ball along with
international, national, and local politicians, have
helped make it a classic old-time Chicago place
to dine. The family-owned and run restaurant proudly
boasts a legion of regular customers, some going back
more than 50 years.

Paperwhite Studio were inspired by the rich history
of the brand and worked with the family to revive
the brand by bringing back vintage graphic elements
paired with modern typography and illustrations.

GENE & GEORGETTI
G & G
19 41
STEAKHOUSE

WHISKEY
ON THE ROCKS

The gentlemen's way

Ollie's Burger

Cherry Bomb Creative Co. / cherrybomb.com.mx

"Imagine being in a noisy, overflowing cafeteria, looking out the window at the big, fast cars speeding down the street, while the man in the booth across enjoys his breakfast and in a carefree manner flips through his newspaper. You, with the natural curiosity of a child, pay attention to the news photos, where strange men appear, all dressed in fluffy white suits, who make you dream of yourself crossing in your spaceship at full speed (just like the fast cars behind the window), the immense darkness of outer space, conquering creatures from distant worlds... when suddenly, the waitress, with the plate's noise colliding with the table, brings your feet back to the ground and you can see in front on you that big, juicy and delicious cheeseburger that you desire so much, accompanied by a giant stack of greasy, hot fries and a delicious vanilla milkshake with a cherry on top. Life is good."

This was the lifelong dream of Cherry Bomb's client. For his new entrepreneurship in his native Kuwait, he decided to set up a dark kitchen that offers the best possible version of the classic, authentic and unpretentious American burger. Cherry Bomb were commissioned to create Ollie's Burger, a brand that seeks to recreate that classic All-American diner aesthetic.

Cherry Bomb decided that they would pay homage to all those children who lived through the era of the space race and who found themselves 'crossing the galaxies' while taking a good bite of their delicious cheeseburger by designing the cute Astro-chubby boy mascot.

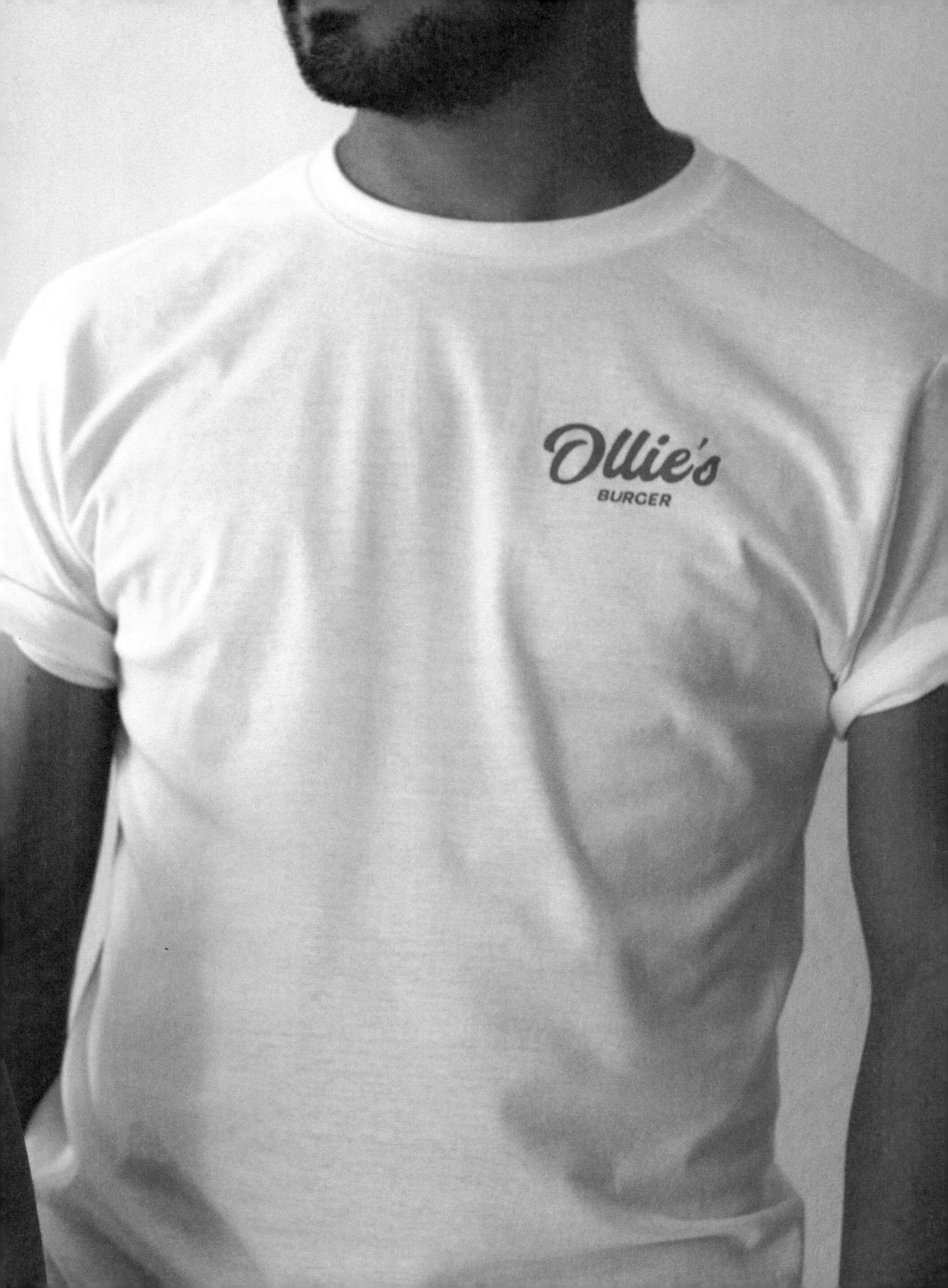
Ollie's
BURGER

By The Bottle

Seachange / seachange.studio

By The Bottle is a small online wine retailer offering a carefully curated selection of sustainable, biodynamic, organic and small-batch wines. They needed a recognisable and approachable identity that could celebrate working with local producers, organic growers and sustainable wine lovers, while also demystifying natural wines, for non-wine-experts.

Seachange developed a hero brand character who is naturally playful, fluid, free-flowing and organic in form, drawn to be a neutral personification of people who love all things wine-related. The sculptural style of the illustrations play with overlapping, and positive and negative space making them feel like an oddly playful Cubist sketch.

A highly distinct colour palette was utilised, alluding to the colours of natural wine; the pale purple for the bloom on grapes and the vivid red for the bold hues found in many natural wines.

✌ Seachange developed a hero brand character who is naturally playful, fluid, free—flowing and organic in form. ✌

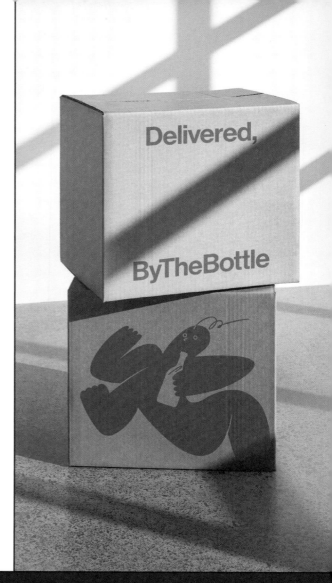

Yaki

Old Friend / oldfriend.co

Yaki is a food truck in Waco, Texas that blends the tried-and-true teriyaki combo meal with oak-smoked Texas BBQ.

The brand communicates a simple meal that is approachable and satisfying to all customers. Old Friend's creation of what would later be dubbed the 'SOSS BOSS' introduces each delicious meal with a friendly face.

SMOKED WITH OAK

SOSS BOSS

I ♥ YAKI

TEXAS STYLE

YAKI TO-GO

Enjoy!

SOSS BOSS

Thank you!

YAKI
TEXAS TERIYAKI

Thank you!

Enjoy!

YAKI TO-GO

SMOKED WITH OAK

TEXAS STYLE

Enjoy!

YAKI

I ♥ YAKI

👌 **Old Friend's creation of what would later be dubbed the 'SOSS BOSS' introduces each delicious meal with a friendly face.** 👌

Dumpling Darlings

Foreign Policy Design Group / foreignpolicy.design

A dumpling bar with a twist, designed to break the mould of stereotypical Asian joints. The brand's visual language is largely inspired by the Japanese manga found in Shokudo (casual Japanese eateries), with storylines based on a main character Jo and her pet pig, Pork Chop.

The logotype is also inspired by the vertical writing system and characteristic calligraphic quality of traditional Kanji. The contrasting mix of bright, electric colours is used to layer a pop treatment and youthful appeal to the brand. The interior design continues the visual language of a Shokudo, translated into a casual bar with cosy lighting and tongue-in-cheek graphics in various corners. The lights and canvas at the bar counter are both inspired by the intricate folds of dumplings.

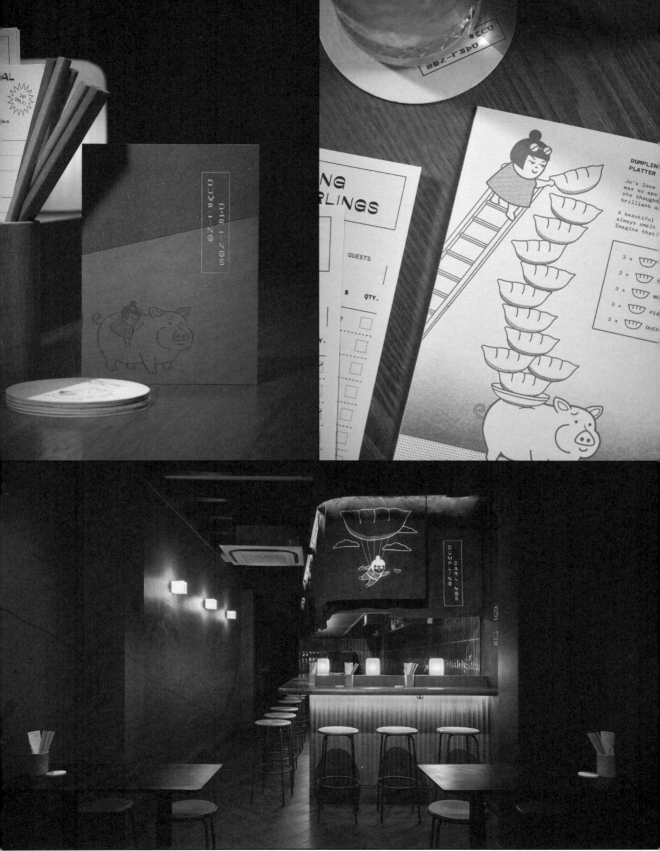

👆 **The brand's visual language is largely inspired by the Japanese manga found in Shokudo (casual Japanese eateries).** ✌️

LUNCH SET

Eat your feelings away.
Dumpling Darlings will
always be here to hold you.

1 X		EGG NOODLES
1 X		ICED DRINK
5 X		DUMPLINGS

16$

DUMPLING DARLINGS

GUESTS

$ | QTY.

7 | ☐
8 | ☐

QTY.

☑
☐
☐
☑
☐
7 | ☐
8 | ☐
8 | ☐
20 | ☐

5 | ☐

LONGA
OSMANT
PU-ERH

PASSION
FRUIT
GINGER
SODA   6$

BOTTOMLESS
ARTISANAL
HOT TEA   3$

Don Tuch

Human / byhuman.mx

Don Tuch is a fast-food restaurant located in Mexico City. The restaurant is a tribute to Yucatán cuisine, with a playful and relaxed approach. For the brand's identity, Human wanted to convey vintage nostalgia, reinterpreted in a playful way. They used a serif typeface and a vibrant colour palette to convey this balance. Human also created a character named 'Don Tuch', after the restaurant name, to enhance this friendly approach. Reproduction of the branding assets was very important, Human created different sets of stickers and stamps to lower reproduction costs. The result is a unique and friendly approach that welcomes every member of the family to enjoy this delicious food in a more relaxed ambience.

Character Illustrations: Charles Miranda

☝ **Don Tuch is a tribute to Yucatán cuisine, with a playful and relaxed approach.** ✌

Food & Drink

Gulp

Tais Kahatt / taiskahatt.com

Gulp is an everyday chilli oil that gives all your meals the flavour they are missing. The word 'Gulp' as a verb means swallow quickly, and with this condiment it's impossible not to, that is why the illustration reflects exactly that. Inspired by Asian street food graphics, the combination of typography and minimal layout, with the messy illustration and handwritten details represent what the product is all about, street food in a jar.

Quinby's

After Hours / afterhoursstudio.com.au

Inspired by the tale of Moses Quinby, the famous NYC beekeeper who paved the way for modern-day apiculture, After Hours created an unpretentious and playful identity for Quinby's – a beloved chilli honey brand from Sydney, Australia.

Moses' story informed every aspect of the brand, from the name to the brandmark: a contemporary illustration of the man himself. Breaking away from traditional honey aesthetics of soft florals, the wordmark and supporting typography drew inspiration from Brooklyn signage, instilling the identity with a classic NYC deli feel, while paying homage to Moses' roots.

Pick up a bottle at a good deli near you.

Krüx

Mariela Mezquita / marielamezquita.com
Krüx Döner Kebab was opened from a desire to bring authentic Berliner street food to Mexico City. Through the graphic identity, Mariela Mezquita and Krüx wanted to give an easy, un-anecdotal experience for customers, as casual and mundane as making a pit stop for a döner kebab in Berlin after a party.

To accomplish this, they aimed to make a fun character, like the ones used in traditional restaurants. They took inspiration in the shape of the döner kebab itself, as it resembled a big talking mouth. They added eyes, limbs, a cap and Krüx's mascot was born.

👌 **Through the identity, Mariela Mezquita and Krüx wanted to give an easy, un–anecdotal experience for customers, as casual and mundane as making a pit stop for a döner kebab in Berlin after a party.** 👌

DÖNER
KEBAB
DÖNER KEB
NER KEBA
KEBA
BAB DÖNE
R KEBAB

KEBAB
55 71597117
Calle Rio

55-7159-7117

KRÜX

Calle Rio de Janeiro, Num. 8
Roma Norte, CDMX.

* ORDENA DESDE
RAPPI Y UBEREATS

® KRUXKEBAB
55 71597117

Calle Rio de Janeiro 8, Roma Norte, CDMX

KRÜX
DÖNER KEBAB

KEBAB CORDE
1/2 KEBAB PO
KEB

RÜX
Roma Norte, CDMX
DÖNER KEBAB
$80
ESA $15
$22
$55
$45
ATE
PACÍFICO
$337

Alec Tear

Alec Tear
alectear.com

① The Mean Tomato mascot by Alec Tear and Dan Woodger

Q What is your background and how did you get involved in graphic design?

A   I suppose I originally became involved in graphic design at college. I'd always known I liked to draw and make things, but it wasn't until I started an art foundation course at Hull College of Art and Design that I was required to use those skills to solve a problem, or answer a brief. I've always had an analytical brain, so when I found out that a job existed where I could put my passion for creation to practical use I was hooked.

I then went on to study branding at Northumbria University. Here I learnt how important the conceptual side of graphic design is. We were taught that brilliant execution is, of course, essential, but, if the conceptual foundations aren't in place, then the design can feel hollow or false.

This practiced way of thinking set me up with the skills I needed to land a job in the industry and I quickly found myself working for the acclaimed global design agency Jones Knowles Ritchie. Here I was exposed to working in big creative teams for brands of all shapes and sizes. Over the course of seven years I honed my craft and developed skills in brand creation, packaging design and lettering art.

For the last three years I have been working independently as a designer and lettering artist. I work with a diverse range of clients and creative agencies, spanning many categories of product or service.

The work that I produce still relies on a strong conceptual background, and often leans into my passions for typography and illustration. I absolutely love what I do and take great pleasure in collaborating with others who share my drive for creating great work.

Q How would you describe your creative style and process?

A   I try not to have a creative style as such, although I always try to create work that's accessible for wide audiences (not just designers) to connect with. I don't have much time for design that tries to be too cool for 'regular people'.

Above all else though, I believe that one style doesn't fit all, and that the execution of a project should be driven by what it is trying to achieve. For example: The Mean Tomato ① utilises playful typography and a cheeky cartoon tomato to disarm the consumer and to tap into the nostalgia we all feel towards mischievous cartoon characters from our childhood. Ordering take-away pizza is nearly always a spontaneous purchase and it should feel fun, so it felt right to use a style that didn't take itself too seriously.

On the contrary, my creative process is much more consistent. It always starts with me immersing myself in the brief, and is then followed by a lot of loose sketches, mood boards and (practically incomprehensible) notes to myself. I like to keep these early concepts as unrefined

② Fido Dido, 7up mascot by Joanna Ferrone & Sue Rose

and as open to interpretation as possible. From here, I try to let the best concepts grow organically: meandering through iterative stages of experimentation, collaboration and application. Nothing is set in stone until the last second.

I find that nearly all of my best creative work comes from a directed, but flexible, process like this. And from my experience, it's by far the best way to collaborate between other creatives and clients alike – everyone is given their own space to do what they do best, and can feel collectively responsible for the final output.

Q   What do you think makes a successful mascot?

A   I think the most successful mascots are the ones who become a personification of their brand – they live and breathe them: continuously reminding their audience of who they represent. To achieve this a mascot's physical appearance needs to be extremely distinctive and memorable.

A good mascot should also have the ability to move, gesture, react, interact and generally communicate on a level that a brand alone would not otherwise be able to. A lot of mascots don't have these abilities, and I find it difficult to differentiate them from a regular static logo. In my opinion, a mascot who isn't 'alive' is certainly not being utilised to its fullest potential, and maybe isn't really a mascot at all.

Another way to measure a mascot's success is to look at how long it is used for by the brand. The best mascots are timeless and/or move with the times. They may need to change and evolve – as people and society does. Due to their human-like characteristics, mascots can have a lot of influence, especially with children, so it's essential that they act responsibly; represent human characteristics respectfully; and reflect the changing social expectations of

people. There are countless examples of previously successful mascots who have fallen at these hurdles.

Q   Do you have a favourite mascot and why?

A   I've always been a big fan of 7up's scrawled Fido Dido® – the skating, surfing, hammock lounging chiller. Strangely enough, he didn't start life off as 7up's mascot. He was created by Joanna Ferrone & Sue Rose in 1985 and was stencilled on Tshirts (along with his very own mantra – look it up) which became popular in New York before he was licensed to PepsiCo in 1988.

Although he wasn't designed specifically for selling soft drinks, his laid-back personality was a perfect match for the brand. Growing up in the 90s, I remember Fido Dido showing-up across loads of 7up packaging and merch, and his presence alone always made everything look so effortlessly cool. He really brought a lot, 7up don't utilise him as much as they could do these days!

Q   We've been using mascots in branding for the last 100 years, why do you think they have stood the test of time?

A   I think mascots have stood the test of time because they're such a powerful branding device. They're essentially walking, talking ambassadors for brands, and a great way of delivering a personality to a product or service that might not instinctively have one. The Michelin man is a brilliant example of this – who would have thought a tyre brand could be so charismatic? Similarly, mascots give brands the ability to add emphasis or expression to brand messaging, in the same way that adding an emoji to the end of a sentence works.

However, I think the underlying reason that mascots have stood the test of time is because they're so relatable. Brands,

③ The Mean Tomato mascot by
Alec Tear and Dan Woodger

especially the big ones, can often come across as soulless entities, but having a mascot can soften that, giving the brand a friendly face to focus on. We humans are hardwired to recognise and remember faces, we can do this as soon as we can see. As babies we instinctively know to look people in the eyes, and even as adults we spot faces in the clouds that aren't even there – it's just how our brains are wired. And if the goal of a brand is to be recognised and remembered, then what better way to do it than by giving it a face?

Q   What was your experience with designing one of your mascots?

A   In the case of The Mean Tomato, ® the process of styling the tomato was quite a smooth one, however a lot of time was spent beforehand in defining his personality traits. Nailing these was essential, as they'd go on to form the creative brief.

Of course, the tomato needed to be mean – but we also decided that he should be cheeky, witty, absolutely full of himself, but most importantly, still lovable. There is a lot of visual nuance in this mix of personality traits, so we commissioned the best in the cartoon business, Dan Woodger (represented by Jelly). I had admired Dan's delightfully squishy style for a long time and had been waiting for a project that would be the perfect fit for him.

Dan and I worked together closely during the creative process, and he was an amazing guy to collaborate with. There was a lot of passing back and forth of sketches where we explored the tomato's anatomy, body language and facial expressions – it's amazing to see how tweaking just one of these things can change the overall character of a mascot.

My favourite part of this fine tuning process was all of the unusual discussions that come with it: such as, 'what should a mean tomato's hair look like?' The answer

to this one was – 'spiky' – for the same reason that Dennis the Menace, Bart Simpson and Rick Sanchez have spiky hair, because it adds attitude and grit. Careful considerations like this went into each and every element of our mascot, and I think this level of thinking is essential when creating a character that exudes personality.

Q   Do you have any specific hopes for how this mascot will develop in the future?

A   I can't wait to see how other creatives interpret The Mean Tomato. I'd love to see him animated in commercials, maybe even in 3D? And I've always wondered what his voice might sound like. In preparation for this kind of activation we created an in-depth personality guideline outlining exactly how he should behave (or not behave, I suppose).

As he develops over time, my main hope for him is that he remains properly mean and doesn't just end up being another brand cheer leader. Every brand mascot has a unique personality, but historically they're always pretty cheery – because what brand wouldn't want to be perceived in that way? The interesting thing about The Mean Tomato as a mascot is that he intentionally clashes with the brand, calling them out on their expected brand BS and generally causing havoc. This is a much more memorable way for a mascot to act and it opens up some really unexpected storytelling opportunities for the brand. I look forward to seeing what he gets up to in the future!

The Mean Tomato

Alec Tear / alectear.com

The take-out pizza category is an extremely crowded one. Pretty much everything that can be said about pizza has been said, and it's becoming increasingly hard for brands to break through the cheesy noise... Enter The Mean Tomato – created exclusively for delivery service Gopuff. In order to stand out, Alec Tear, working with Kuba & Friends, knew he needed to create a pizza brand that acted a little differently. So, although this brand leans into a lot of the classic NY pizzeria tropes, the brand mascot certainly does not. Rather than bringing yet another 'Gr-r-reat' overly enthusiastic mascot into the world, they took a more unexpected approach and created one who could work a bit harder for the brand, or not, depending on how you look at it.

Illustrations: Dan Woodger

Sleazy Pizza

Another Kind Studio / anotherkind.co.uk

Another Kind Studio were approached by The Truman Brewery team to create a new pizza brand for a vacant restaurant space within their East London complex.

After several research and consultation sessions with the team they came up with a concept that would take design influences from vintage erotica, modern day cartoon illustrations and incorporate pun-tastic copy in to what would eventually become the deliciously naughty Sleazy Pizza brand.

Design and Illustrations: Patrick Perring

Caferría

PAZ MIAMOR / pazmiamor.com

Caferría is the combination of a specialty coffee shop and a seller of fresh products from local fairs, located in Córdoba, Argentina. Its identity reflects an urban spirit that represents a relaxed consumer experience.

The graphic identity was inspired by the stamps used on takeaway cups, utilising their colour and detail to complete the rest of the design applications.

It is a simple but dynamic system, made of well-contrasted fonts and coffee cup illustrations, characterised by everyday situations. It results in a cheerful and easy-to-use identity.

Eddie's Deli

Half Decent / halfdecent.studio

Eddie's Deli is a food truck based on the east coast of Australia. The visual identity utilises intentionally stretched logos, stylised motion, and ambiguous photo usage. The design system finds balance through an earthy colour palette, playful illustrations and thought-provoking taglines.

The truck offers toasted sandwiches, so Half Decent dissected that idea and broke out individual food groups to help form the basis of the system. 'Toasty' the mascot is the brand advocate and is used to help liven the brand's personality.

The logotype and Toasty are both custom drawn and uniquely 1-of-1's for Eddie's food truck.

'Toasty' the mascot is the brand advocate and is used liven the brand's personalit

The Club Sandwich

Karla Heredia / karlaheredia.com
The Club Sandwich is not a secret club, it is for everyone.

A meeting with friends or an outing to the park to take a break and enjoy. The graphic communication is literally represented by 'a sandwich club'. Its mascots are presented in groups and individually through communication and applications, accompanied by patterns that simulate a picnic tablecloth, giving a feeling of fraternity and fun.

Considering that since there is no establishment, the packaging is the face of the company and how the product is presented. Its bold and enjoyable visual identity has been created with easy application and reproduction in mind.

THE SANDWICH CLUB

THE SANDWICH CLUB

SANDWICH LOVERS UNITE

THE SANDWICH CLUB

Your sandwich fillings:
2 Unleashed Dog
3 Santa Mortadella

TOTAL: £26,00
FOR: Kurt

If you felt the love don't keep it yourself.
Share it @thesandwichclubuk

★ ENJOY ★
www.thesandwichclub.uk
London, UK

tsc

NOT A SECRET CLUB

SANDWICH LOVERS UNITE

THE SANDWICH CLUB

Your sandwich fillings:
Posh Caprese
Unleashed Dog
Santa Mortadella

TOTAL: £17,00
FOR: HANS

If you felt the love don't keep it yourself.
Share it @thesandwichclubuk.

★ ENJOY ★
www.thesandwichclub.uk
London, UK

tsc

THE SANDWICH CLUB

www.thesandwichclub.uk
@thesandwichclubuk
★ London, UK ★

tsc

NOT
A SECRET
CLUB

THE
SANDWICH
CLUB

THE
SANDWICH
CLUB

www.thesandwic
@thesandwic
★ Londo

Welcome sandwich lovers!

Receive sandwiches,
promotions and surprises.

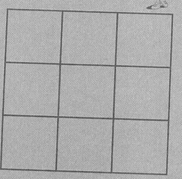

If you felt the love don't keep it yourself.
Share it @thesandwichclubuk

★ ENJOY ★

THE
SANDWICH
CLUB

www.thesandwichclub.uk
@thesandwichclubuk
★ London, UK ★

tsc

THE
SANDWICH
CLUB

tsc
The
Sandwich
Club

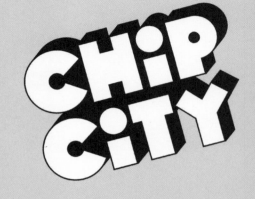

Chip City

Paperwhite Studio / paperwhite-studio.com
Chip City approached Paperwhite Studio with an
opportunity to rethink and expand its brand – to new
storefronts across the city, and a food truck, as well
as into a direct-to-consumer business that ships
ready to bake cookies straight to your door.

To transport customers to Chip City, Paperwhite Studio
created a delightful world where everything the brand
touched became a little more whimsical, a little more
fun, and a whole lot sweeter.

From there, they worked to infuse a sense of youthful,
joy-filled style into every touchpoint, balancing bright,
quirky cookie mascot illustrations and a vintage type
style with enticing photography and a casual approach
to messaging.

Have a Gooey Day!

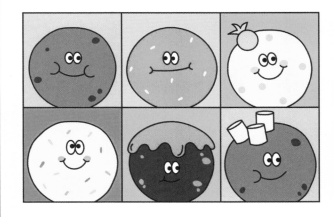

CHIP CITY

Claytony's Pizza Palace

Steve Gavan / stevegavan.work
Claytony's Pizza Palace is an exclusive pizzeria run out of the back of a house in Hawthorndene,
South Australia. A simple brief entailed creating a fun, friendly and classic brand to communicate
Claytony's delicious and authentic pizzas.

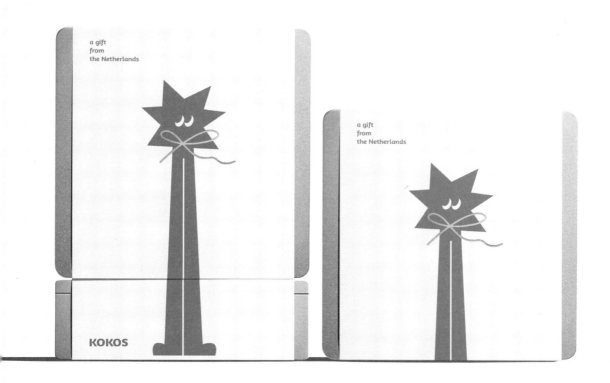

KOKOS

Lung-Hao Chiang / behance.net/st60701
KOKOS, means coconut in Dutch (yes, the founder loves coconut). The brand identity and packaging design use the image of a coconut as a mascot, which hopes to echo KOKOS's passion for food, offer a 'human touch' and an emotional feeling.

Due to the COVID-19 epidemic, the desire to travel to other countries became more difficult. Lung-Hao Chiang explored the concept of, 'taking everyone to the Netherlands with your taste buds' into the biscuit gift box. There are eight types of biscuit, representing the Netherlands' different provinces, various festivals and a little history and culture.

When people are in the store the warm aroma of baking cookies is like the Netherlands in winter.

👌 **The brand identity and packaging design use the image of a coconut as a mascot, which hopes to echo KOKOS's passion for food, offer a 'human touch' and an emotional feeling.** ✌️

Pizza Bear

Atsushi Hirano (AFFORDANCE inc.) / affordance.tokyo
Twenty freshly baked cookies can be found inside these pizza boxes. The idea for the branding came from the unusual but tasty pizza flavour they had. The aim of the design was for it to be as bright as possible, to convey the atmosphere of that flavour. The cuteness of the line-drawn teddy bear, combined with the thought of comforting pizza makes for a nostalgic and approachable identity.

✌️ **The cuteness of the line–drawn teddy bear, combined with the thought of comforting pizza makes for a nostalgic and approachable identity.** ✌️

Animals

MONTELUPO

BY

RALLENTI PASTA

MONTELUPO

3
44

NE
28

ITALIAN MARKET

Montelupo

Old Friend / oldfriend.co

Montelupo Italian restaurant and market is the newest creation from Portland restaurateur Adam Berger. Montelupo or 'Mountain of the Wolf' provided the inspiration for a canine-led identity, with typography inspired by old Italian signage.

In conjunction with the restaurant, Montelupo has its own line of boxed pasta, wine, beer and coffee. Old Friend made sure that the design system was simple and flexible enough to feel recognisable across products while avoiding repetition.

MONTELUPO

BY
RALLENTI PASTA

MADE IN
PORTLAND

CAVATAPPI

BRONZE
DIE-CUT

MADE WITH
SHEPHERD'S GRAIN DURUM WHEAT

NET WT. 16 OZ (1 LB.) 454G

LOI

HOMI / ho-mi.ch

LOI is a new vegetarian bistro in Zürich which is located in a former beer brewery called Löwenbräu. The Lion, in German 'Löwe' and in Swiss German 'LOI', is the city symbol and gave the beer its name. However the Löwenbräu brewery shut its doors in the mid 80s.

For a few years the building had been used as an art center, retaining its old name of Löwenbräu, renting out its space to galleries and museums.

HOMI were asked to design the visual identity for the bistro, which functions as an extended museum café. In the tradition of many restaurants they decided to work with a mascot, that of a lion, which would be the center of the visual identity. Visually, HOMI wanted the lion to make a connection to the building's new function as an art center. So they teamed up with the artist and illustrator Olga Prader. Together they defined the look and style of the mascot and Olga Prader took the lion further by illustrating it in different roles. For example: the lion drinking, resting, serving food, etc.

Over time, the identity will grow and develop as HOMI and Olga Prader make more illustrations for new situations. The illustrations are paired with the typeface Ionic from Monotype which has similarities to the old logo from the beer brewery.

Karla Heredia

Karla Heredia
karlaheredia.com

Q What is your background and how did you become involved in graphic design?

A   I have always been attracted to visual expression and appreciation. I am interested in art, aesthetics, communication, architecture, culture and history and I find that everything that attracts me comes together in design. I studied graphic design, and I decided to focus on branding. I love to learn about each project I develop, each of them is a different story, requiring new knowledge, different concepts and offering an independent adventure.

Q How would you describe your creative style and process?

A   I like to research, analyze and then simplify the idea based on a concept in an aesthetic and functional way. I love to contrast and incorporate mixed techniques, as well as illustrations and patterns, to achieve a functional and moldable design result. Through this approach, I'm trying to provide the brand with recognizable and attractive elements, based on a strong concept of cultural influence.

Q What do you think makes a successful mascot?

A   Mascots are the concept of a brand synthesized in a character, they are its communication and often the 'guy' that brings a smile to the public's face. I think they should have a strong personality and communicate the style and attitude of the brand, as well as being funny in some way. They also need to adapt to the communication style of the brand they represent.

Q Do you have a favourite mascot and why?

A   Not one in particular, but I love that brands are accompanied with mascots, I feel very attracted to them. It seems to me a unique, representative and memorable way to communicate. I think mascots are an extension/complementary graphic that allows us to know more about the essence and personality of the brand.

Q We've been using mascots in branding for the last 100 years, why do you think they have stood the test of time?

The Sandwich Club mascot
by Karla Heredia

CAFE 3/92 mascot
by Karla Heredia

Because they are beautiful, fun and allow the public to have a knowledge beyond the brand. Mascots provide a sense of personification to which we can identify its attributes and values in a simple way.

Q   What was your experience with designing your mascots, is it a difficult process?

A   I think it's a challenge. Getting a mascot to reflect the personality of a brand involves creating a whole story behind a concept, focusing the mascot in an imaginary world, incorporating personality, attributes, actions, attitude, through the stroke, style of the character, features, movement, position, etc. And that manages to reflect the sense and feeling that we seek to project, accompanying the brand to another level of communication. On the other hand, personally I find it a very fun process. I like to imagine its story and think about what it does. What it wants to say and express. The different ways to represent it and incorporate it visually with the rest of the graphic elements of the brand are very important.

Q   What are your main goals and considerations when working on a mascot?

A   The mascot needs to be incorporated in a very natural and positive way to the rest of the brand, becoming an integral part of it and not as an external element that just accompanies it. In addition, it should communicate the brand's attributes and values in a simple and quick way, avoiding confusing the viewer.

Q   How can a mascot enhance a brand?

A   A mascot should feel part of the brand and communicate or express the brand's personality. If it doesn't feel that way, if it has nothing to say, or communicates it in the wrong way, the best idea may be to restructure or eliminate it.

Make its presence add to the brand's visual communication, not subtract.

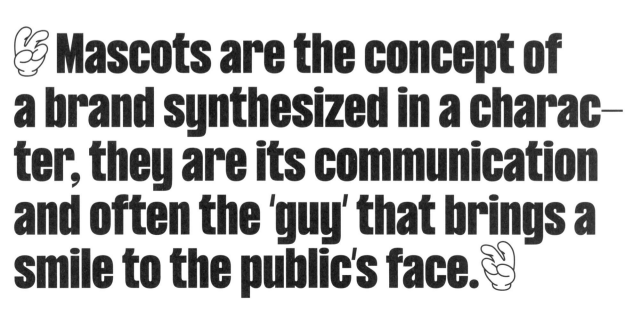

Mascots are the concept of a brand synthesized in a character, they are its communication and often the 'guy' that brings a smile to the public's face.

CAFE 3/92

Karla Heredia / karlaheredia.com
CAFE 3/92 is a coffee shop located in Mexico. With an outgoing and fun personality, the character of the brand is the center of the visual image. The CAFE 3/92 mascot is a fox who drinks a lot of coffee, has a good time, is carefree and wanders everywhere.

The identity design is intended to be easy to use, over multiple applications, giving strength to the personality of the mascot and livening up the environment.

The CAFE 3/92 mascot is a fox who drinks a lot of coffee, has a good time, is carefree and wanders everywhere.

KKVEL

DESIGN DESIGN Inc. / designdesign.jp
DESIGN DESIGN Inc. were in charge of the visual identity design for KKVEL, a wood-fired oven restaurant and home-roasted coffee shop that opened in Sanjo City, Niigata Prefecture. DESIGN DESIGN Inc. were in charge of the store name, concept, logo, product packaging, aprons, tote bags, opening announcement tools, flyers, signage planning, photo direction, and web direction. They named the store 'KKVEL' after the process of wood-firing.

The concept of the store is 'My Pace, Slow Life'. The motif of the logo is a turtle walking slowly, to reflect this and their sustainable concept that reduces food loss as much as possible. The large turtle represents the wood fired oven and the small turtle represents the coffee beans.

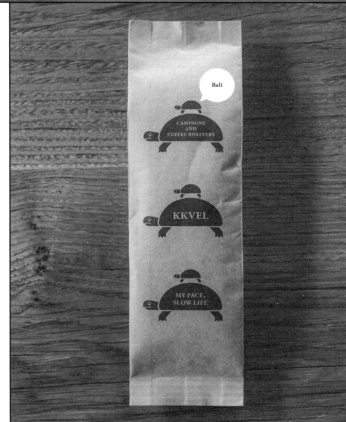

Bandit

Valen Lim / behance.net/valenlim
Bandit is a small neighbourhood café, serving a curated selection of drinks and baked goods in Kuala Lumpur. Their raccoon mascot is a wink to the cafe's name, meant to evoke the brand's youth and playfulness. The black mask, worn by this playful partner-in-crime, is designed to mimic the silhouette of a freshly-baked loaf of bread.

Fun taglines, peppered with puns, were created to complement the above, such as 'ban(appe)dit', 'wearetroublebakers' and 'trouble's a brewin'. The menu also unfolds to become an eye mask, complete with strategically-placed cutouts, a fun interactive element to drive home the cafe's brand.

BANDIT

👌 **The black mask, worn by this playful partner–in–crime, is designed to mimic the silhouette of a freshly–baked loaf of bread.** ✌️

The Grateful Pet

Foreign Policy Design Group / foreignpolicy.design

The tale of The Grateful Pet began in 2017, when an animal-loving duo set off to uncover the best blends for their best friends. Four years in, they were ready to launch a wider range of premium food for both cats and dogs, and needed a fresh, confident identity to boot.

Through vibrant illustrations, celebratory colours and lively slogans that match those four-legged attitudes, Foreign Policy Design Group developed a brand identity that's as unforgettable as the animals we love.

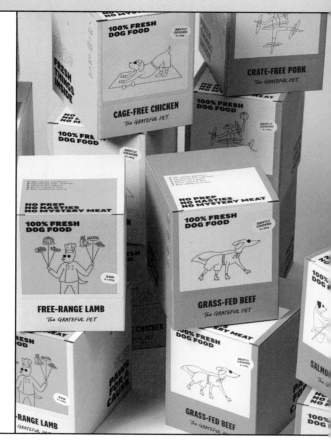

CRATE-FREE PORK

The GRATEFUL PET

100% FRESH DOG FOOD

GENTLY COOKED
8 x 250g

SALMON & SARDINE

The GRATEFUL PET

PAWS FOR A CAUSE

100% FRESH DOG FOOD

MEAT

GRASS-FED VENISON

The GRATEFUL PET

A portion of each sale
goes towards The Grateful
Give Back, our fund for
partner animal shelters

PAWS FOR A CAUSE

DOG FOOD

RAW
8 x 250g

Soulfly

Paperwhite Studio / paperwhite-studio.com

Soulfly is dedicated to serving up the best classic fried chicken with a twist. Since opening their food truck in Miami in 2021, Soulfly has continued to grow into physical locations, bringing people together with their unique mix of local hospitality and delicious comfort food.

Paperwhite Studio drew inspiration from the brand's hip hop roots, vintage fast food aesthetics, and paired it with a too-cool brand mascot. As a result, a bold and lovable identity was born.

OUR BREAD & BUTTER

TASTE OF THE SOUTH $12
Boneless Breast, Vinegar Slaw, Tomato, Pickles, ComeBack Sauce

BIRD ON THE RUN $12
Boneless Breast dipped in hot spice oil

CROP BURGER $14
Oyster muhroom, butter, lettuce, tomato, pickles, comeback sauce

DELICIOUS!

BIRD ON FIRE $14
TOO HOT
Boneless Breast, Calabrian Chili Mayo, Pickles, Fly Sauce

FLY WINGS $10
8 Breaded Wings, Goldie Sauce

SIDES

THE MAC $6		**SLAW** $6	
Creamy Macaroni		Vinegar Seasoned Cabbage	
SPUDS $6		**SMOKED GREENS** $6	
Freshly Cut Fries		Braised Collard Greens	
DIRTY RICE $6		**FRIED CORN** $6	

Tingling **Soulfly**

MAKE IT FLY

HOT & SPICY

KOSHER STYLE!

CRUNCH & SPICE
Everything nice

Canine Cleanup

Loki Creative / weareloki.com

Canine Cleanup is an initiative by Wanderruff, a sustainable dog accessories brand focused on using recycled and organic materials. Canine Cleanup was unveiled as part of Earth Month 2022 to encourage dog owners to be kind to Mother Earth by picking up a new daily habit of litter-picking while on their dog walks.

Mascot Ruffus Cleanright spearheads the campaign. Ruffus was created as campaign mascot to connect and engage with the Wanderruff army of eco-conscious dog owners.

MASCOT: RUFFUS CLEANRIGHT

CANINE CLEANUP

UserZoom

How&How / how.studio

How&How's rebrand for UserZoom breathed wisdom and warmth into the leading UX insights platform. They repositioned and relaunched the multi-national user experience software and service company as the world's most complete UX research solution.

How&How's research told them the existing brand and owl mascot (affectionately known as 'Zooie') were not meeting the expectations of their customers – and were in fact negatively impacting their position in the market. So they gave Zooie a facelift and updated the design language to be warm yet wise, leveraging the gentle softness of the Recoleta typeface to provide something familiar yet fresh. The brand was expanded into a full illustrated and animated icon package, and applied to extensive company collateral.

Bean So Good

Lung-Hao Chiang / behance.net/st60701

The Lunar New Year is the most important holiday for Chinese people all over the world. No matter how difficult life is or how many troubles they have, they will be healed in the atmosphere of the Lunar New Year, full of blessings and warmth during the period. However, under the influence of COVID-19, many changes have taken place in our lives and people are in a depressed state of mind. As such, this Chinese New Year packaging design, for the Year of the Tiger, combines fun and humour to bring a relaxed and happy feeling to consumers. The casual graffiti style is utilised in the illustration style and excessive structure, such as rationality and geometry, is reduced. Since this year is the Year of the Tiger in the Lunar New Year, the concept of the tiger is interpreted as a lucky cat, which symbolises blessings and wealth for consumers. It also suggests a cat's laziness – its postures wishing everyone a leisurely and relaxing Chinese New Year.

P ∞

Linda Jukic

Accompany
accompany.group

Q What is your background and how did you become involved in graphic design?

A I was interested in visual design at school. It was a natural progression to study Visual Communication Design at University. Following my studies I kicked-off my career at a studio focused on branding and graphic design and have continued this focus from there on.

Q How would you describe your creative style and process?

A Accompany was founded on the principle that brands are owned by clients and we are joining their leadership team for a period of time as an expert on strategic branding and design.

Our approach to branding is entirely focused on creating one-of-a-kind identities that disrupt attention, communicate purpose and drive intentional action. We lead with intelligence and humility, knowing that by developing understanding we can shape design that is meaningful and effective.

Our approach is uncomplicated, allowing insights and ideas to emerge to create distinctive and effective outcomes. We work with our clients to reveal an ownable point of view and create authentic brand identities that engage with the world and people.

Q What do you think makes a successful mascot?

A Recognisability, meaningfulness and personality. In the sense that a viewer can identify and connect with

They're visual shortcuts in brand storytelling, an insignia for a business's personality and attributes.

① Stanford Brown mascot
by Accompany

Puppy Matters Co. mascot
by Accompany

it, whether it be with its visual form or with its metaphorical, associative or suggestive qualities. It genuinely captures compelling qualities of a business, offers a unique take on the world and connects with the heads and hearts of its audience. If it does these well, it becomes relatable and ultimately memorable. I love that the most successful of mascots transcend business symbols and become cultural icons.

Q We've been using mascots in branding for the last 100 years, why do you think they have stood the test of time?

A Branding came about as a commercial tool. In its most pure form, it emerged as a practice focused on creating a symbol that a product, service, business could be identified, recalled and remembered by.

Mascots typically tap into the familiar. Known creatures and characters that embody certain qualities. They're visual shortcuts in brand storytelling, an insignia for a business's personality and attributes. I believe they've stood the test of time as they tap into the timeless and universal language of storytelling and personality traits. And as branding is about connecting a person to a business, there's nothing more powerful than playing into these enduring human basics.

Q What was your experience with designing the Stanford Brown mascot, was it a difficult process?

A Generally I have found mascot design can be polarising. Some clients absolutely love the idea of being able to distill their business's qualities through a representational character which their business can get behind. Others find the idea too visually layered, perhaps even too emotive, personality driven, even risky.

During the ideation stage of Stanford Brown ® we thought an animal mascot could be a great way for us to embody many of the qualities the business identified themselves with. Most of the team were financial advisers and accountants with strong corporate backgrounds so we were a little concerned with how it would fly with them – would they think it was too out there?

We realised there were two ways for us to inspire them. Firstly, that they genuinely were seeking a way to stand-out from the corporate crowd so they needed to do something a little unconventional for the category, and secondly, the elephant was logical in its representation. We needed to capture 'tough love' and the elephant is not only one of the strongest creatures, but also one of the most nurturing and emotionally intelligent.

Critical to the process was demonstrating an elephant embodied all the right personality, that we could hit the right balance between professionalism and playfulness. As such, the style and details of the elephant became the focus. Ensuring it felt sophisticated in its aesthetic, and then looking at all the details from the size of the ears and trunk, to the movement of the legs, tail and trunk and even the expression of its eyes and mouth. We worked through all the attributes in detail with our client to ensure we hit the right note.

Q How can a good mascot enhance a brand?

A Above all, a mascot enhances a brand through its ability to express personality, and its this personality which enhances the opportunity for people to connect with a brand. If done well, not only do the staff get behind the mascot, but customers and clients do as well. And in some cases, this unifying of people can lead to micro-movements inspired by the qualities the mascot embodies.

Stanford Brown

Accompany / accompany.group

Stanford Brown, a private wealth company, are known for going deeper on the things that matter and providing expertise that fulfill clients' lives. The anchor of the new identity is an elephant. One of the strongest and most emotionally intelligent creatures, the elephant made for the perfect embodiment of Stanford Brown's tough love ethos.

With rich greens, metaphorical illustrations, natural photography and compelling messages, the new brand captures Stanford Brown's warmth and intelligence, and ensures they stand out of the corporate crowd.

Dear Steven,

It was a pleasure meeting you.

We thought you would be interested in this thought piece we've written.

Look forward to working with you.

Vincent O'Neill

StanfordBrown

Dale Jefferson
Head of Accounting

T.   +61 2 9204 1356
M. +61 412 734 029
E.   d.jefferson@stanfordbrown.com.au
W. stanfordbrown.com.au
A.   Level 8, 15 Blue Street
      North Sydney NSW 2060

StanfordBrown Private Wealth

Puppy Matters Co.

Accompany / accompany.group

Puppy Matters Co. is a start-up business that offers an alternative to the usual tricks and treats puppy teaching approach. Believing that each and every pup is unique and deserves a learning approach especially suited to them and their puppy parents, Accompany created a business name and wordmark that puts puppies first. Referencing the 'PM' initials of the brand name, Accompany created a set of charming puppy characters in all shapes and sizes to work alongside the wordmark and show that all puppies do matter. Proud and purposeful, the brand's a perfect balance of pat-able personality and crafted simplicity.

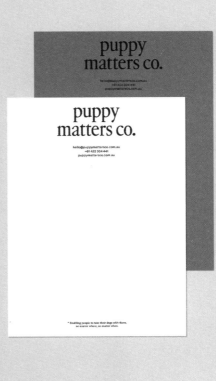

We Compost

Seachange / seachange.studio
Feed the worms! We Compost are a leading compost collection service in New Zealand.

The identity celebrates the mighty worm (worms play a crucial role in composting). The iconic worm logo is modern and playful and speaks to the grass-roots of composting. Seachange extended this into a bespoke typeface 'Worms Display', as well as a bold graphic worm print for maximum stand-out.

Given the hugely positive impact composting has on our earth, it was important for Seachange to create an engaging and educational brand that would appeal to everyone (not just the eco-warriors).

This business card
will biodegrade
in 10 weeks

Gemma Spring

021 155 5250
0800 932 667
gemma@wecompost.co.nz
wecompost.co.nz

The iconic worm logo is modern and playful and speaks to the grass–roots of compost–ing. Seachange extended this into a bespoke typeface 'Worms Display'.

A–to–Z of Composting

A Apples

b Bamboo skewers

C Coffee grounds

D Dough

e Egg cartons

F Feijoas

G Grass clippings

h Hamburgers

I Ice cream

J Jelly

K Kumara

L Lunch box leftovers

M Moldy bread

N Noodles

O Orange peels

P Pizza boxes

Q Quinoa

R Rice

S Shells

T Toilet paper rolls

U Uncoated paper

V Vegetables

W Watermelon rind

X Xmas trees

y Yoghurt

Z Zucchini

WE COMPOST

35L bin

This bag is certified compos~~table~~
in both home and commerci~~al~~
compost systems.

wecompost.co.nz

This product meets EN13432 standard for compostability.

WARNING: To avoid danger of suffocation, keep this bag away from bab~~ies~~

bin liner

~~cer~~tified compostable
~~a~~nd commercial
~~syste~~ms.

~~.co~~.nz

~~for~~ compostabili~~ty~~

Seoul Record Fair

Studio fnt / studiofnt.com

Seoul Record Fair is the first local sale event to embody record labels, musicians, and music fans. Studio fnt have been in charge of this for the past ten years. Their task was to art direct the visual language and graphics of the entire event. In 2016, when the event entered the sixth episode, they created a mascot and named it Reco-nyang (Nyang is an expression that means cat in Korean). Jaemin Lee of Studio fnt collaborated with designer Jisung Park to make this mascot. Not just cute but somewhat suspicious and eccentric, this cat is increasingly loved by visitors who have visited the Seoul Record Fair for years. They intended that Reco-nyang would add richness to the visual elements of the event design identity. It also sought to create profits through the sale of mascot-related products.

Art direction and graphic design: Jaemin Lee
Character design: Jisung Park
Souvenir design: Jisung Park and Jaemin Lee

LIMITED EDITIONS

2016 서울레코드페어 한정반
❶ 강아솔 〈정직한 마음〉
❷ 갤럭시 익스프레스 〈WALKING ON EMPTY〉

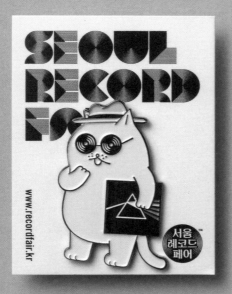

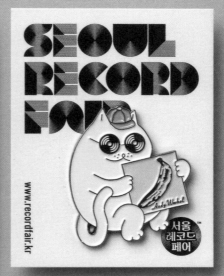

Not just cute but somewhat suspicious and eccentric, this cat is increasingly loved by visitors.

Michael Joseph

Mother Design / motherdesign.com

Founded in 1935, and joining Penguin in 1985, Michael Joseph has a long and distinguished history of publishing the very best authors in each field and bringing their books to the widest possible audience.

The core of the new brand is the mermaid emblem – used in a range of lockups as well as in the colophon on all book spines – which captures the heritage of Michael Joseph in a refreshing contemporary style. A punchy, aquatic jade serves as the brand's primary colour, inspired by the division's maverick, future-facing personality.

☝ **The core of the new brand is the mermaid emblem — used in a range of lockups as well as in the colophon on all book spines — which captures the heritage of Michael Joseph in a refreshing contemporary style.** ✌

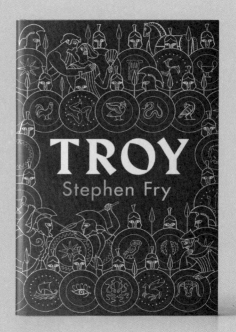

Counter-Print
© 2025 Counter-Print
counter-print.co.uk
info@counter-print.co.uk

ISBN:
978-1-915392-04-6

First published in
the United Kingdom
in 2022. Reprinted
in 2023, 2024 and 2025.

Edited and produced
by Counter-Print.

Design:
Jon Dowling
& Céline Leterme

Cover Illustration:
Yeye Weller

Typefaces:
PP Formula & GT America

Printing and Binding:
1010 Printing International
Limited, China

**British Library
cataloguing-in-
publication data:**
A catalogue of
this book can be found
in the British Library.